The "Faith i
General Editors: Geo
D

MISSION FOR A PILOT

THE STORY OF LEONARD CHESHIRE

R. J. Owen

THE RELIGIOUS EDUCATION PRESS
A Division of Pergamon Press

The Religious Education Press
A Division of Pergamon Press
Hennock Road, Exeter EX2 8RP

Pergamon Press Ltd
Headington Hill Hall, Oxford OX3 0BW

Pergamon Press Inc.
Maxwell House, Fairview Park, Elmsford, New York 10523

Pergamon Press Canada Ltd
Suite 104, 150 Consumers Road, Willowdale, Ontario M2J 1P9

Pergamon Press (Australia) Pty Ltd
P.O. Box 544, Potts Point, N.S.W. 2011

Pergamon Press GmbH
Hammerweg 6, D-6242 Kronberg,
Federal Republic of Germany

Photographs are reproduced by courtesy of The Leonard Chesire Foundation (pp. 6, 17, 20, 21) and the United Kingdom Atomic Energy Authority (p. 10). Cover photograph from a painting by Terence Cuneo by courtesy of Blaze Fine Arts.

Copyright © 1980 R. J. Owen

All rights reserved. No part of this publication may be reproduced, stored in a retrieval system, or transmitted, in any form or by any means, electronic, electrostatic, magnetic tape, mechanical, photocopying, recording or otherwise, without permission in writing from the publishers.

First published 1980

Reprinted 1980, 1982

Printed in Great Britain by A. Wheaton & Co. Ltd, Exeter

ISBN 0 08 024960 4 non net
ISBN 0 08 024961 2 net

MISSION FOR A PILOT

The story of Leonard Cheshire

It was the winter of 1940. Britain was at war. A British bomber was flying over Cologne in Germany. Suddenly there was a terrible flash and roar in front of the pilot. Another crash and a glaring light came from behind him.

The plane lurched. It began to drop towards the ground. A burning smell filled the cockpit. Quickly the pilot tore off his gloves and put on his oxygen mask.

"Have you dropped the bombs yet?" he asked.

There was no answer. Yes, there was. A faint and painful voice: "I've been hit . . . I've been hit."

A figure covered in blood appeared.

"Fire! The petrol tank's on fire!"

"Well, put it out!" snapped the pilot. He did not have time to ask the man how he was or what had happened. He was too busy trying to save the plane from crashing.

The pilot got the plane under control. Instead of turning back, the plane went on towards its target. The bombs were dropped. Two of the crew managed to put out the fire on board. The plane returned to England.

The bomber jerked to a halt on the runway. Some parts of the plane had been shot away. Twisted metal and burn marks could be seen all over it. The radio and some of the controls were not working. Two members of the five-man crew were burned, one very badly.

The pilot who had brought the plane home was only twenty-three years old. His name was Leonard Cheshire.

Early life

Leonard Cheshire was born in September 1917 at Chester. Shortly afterwards, his family moved to Oxford. Leonard's father was very clever, and later became a professor at Oxford University.

In 1936, after leaving school, Leonard went to stay in Germany for a while. He lived with a family in Potsdam. The idea was for him to learn to speak German better. The German whose home he stayed in was Admiral von Reuter. The Admiral was very keen on two things – the sea and Adolf Hitler. He named all of his sons after battleships. All his sons were members of Hitler's Nazi Party.

"Only five per cent of mankind is worth keeping," the Admiral told young Leonard. "The rest should be put down."

Leonard just looked surprised.

"War's a good way of getting rid of the rabble," the Admiral went on. "Don't you agree?"

"No, sir," replied Leonard, "I don't!"

The Admiral just snorted. Clearly he thought that this Englishman was too soft for words.

When he came back from Germany, Leonard went to study at Oxford University. Besides studying, there were many other things he enjoyed doing there. He liked late nights, hard drinking, fast driving and gambling. He liked doing mad things. Once, he kept driving round a roundabout on a main road until his car ran out of petrol. At a party he pretended he could do a magic trick and smashed somebody's watch to bits.

It was at Oxford University, too, that Leonard first had a chance to fly. He joined the Air Squadron there.

"If you want to be sick," said the man teaching him to fly, "please don't mess up the cockpit." Then he added, "Never flown before?"

"No, sir, never."

"Then this should be fun," grinned the man.

"Yes," replied Leonard in a big-headed way, "let's see how well you can fly."

The man thought he would teach this cheeky youth a lesson. He made the plane loop the loop, climb steeply, swerve and then dive suddenly.

"Wonderful!" shouted Leonard.

The man soon realised that his pupil was not going to scare easily and so he gave up trying to frighten him.

The war

Leonard flew a plane himself for the first time in 1937. Later that year he joined the Royal Air Force Volunteer Reserve. He wished he could spend far more of his time flying. He even prayed for war so that his wish could come true.

The war came in 1939. Leonard was still twenty-one years old when the news came. All over the country, people listened to their radios as the Prime Minister, Neville Chamberlain, spoke slowly and seriously: "I have to tell you that this country is at war with Germany."

Leonard was called up to serve as a pilot officer in the R.A.F. He was chosen to be trained as a bomber pilot. He joined 102 Squadron, which was based at Driffield in Yorkshire.

In the summer of 1940 he was sent on his first raid. By this time the German army had captured much of France. The mission was to bomb bridges at Abbeville in France. This was to prevent the German tanks and lorries from crossing the River Somme so easily.

In the plane, the dull and boring sound of the engines was sometimes broken by the crew talking to each other over the intercom. They would often joke and talk about things which were not at all important. As they reached the target, however, the talking was brief and to the point.

"Drop a flare!"

A great red light lit up the sky beneath them.

"There's the River Somme!"

"Somebody's hit the bridge already!"

"Try another bridge! Any bridge will do."

"The north bridge?"

"Fine!"

"We're going in now!"

The north bridge was bombed. The plane returned to Driffield.

Time and again the squadron was sent out. Often they had to

attack targets in Germany. This was much more dangerous. They attacked docks, factories, bridges, runways, radio stations and army buildings. Many of Leonard's friends and fellow-pilots went out in the darkness to Germany and never returned. Most were killed. Some became prisoners of war in Germany. Leonard was one of the lucky ones who came back every time.

It was on one of these raids on Germany that Leonard's plane was hit and set on fire. He went on to the target and dropped the bombs. Then he got the plane back to base. For his action against the enemy and landing his broken plane safely, he was given a medal – the D.S.O. (the Distinguished Service Order).

Bombs away

"Chesh" or "Cheese", as he was nicknamed, was made Wing Commander in 1942 and Group Captain in 1943. At that time, Leonard was the youngest person in the R.A.F. ever to reach that rank. He was only twenty-five years old.

As Group Captain, Leonard's job was to be in charge of the training of bomber pilots. In fact, he disliked this office-type job. He wanted to fly again. He was very pleased when, later in 1943, he was offered the chance to become Wing Commander of 617 Squadron. This was the "Dam Busters" squadron. Leonard was to take the place of a famous pilot called Guy Gibson.

Leonard became an expert at low-level bombing. The object of this was to drop heavy bombs right on target. He thought this method of bombing was much better than bombing a whole area around a target. It meant far less loss of human life.

Later on "Chesh" and his squadron were given a very special job. They had to find and destroy the launching sites of a new German secret weapon called the V3. This was a huge gun, able to fire a 500-pound shell into London every minute.

If the Germans had ever been able to use the V3 it would have been a terrible weapon. The shells reached a height of 60 miles,

Leonard Cheshire as a young man in the R.A.F.

and then dropped suddenly and silently on to their target. There was no way they could be stopped, and even one could have killed many people.

The Germans stored the guns in shelters covered by about 50 feet of concrete to protect them. No bomb on earth could damage them. So a new bomb was invented by a man called Barnes Wallis. It was called "Tallboy" and weighed over 5 tons.

The new bombs were to be dropped at the *side* of the concrete shelters, not *on* them. They were timed to explode only after they had landed. The hope was that they would go down the side of the shelters and blow up the V3s from underneath.

Leonard led the first attack. He had to land a bomb on a target no bigger than 50 yards square, from a height of almost 4 miles, at night. It was very hard to drop bombs right on target from such a great height. However, the attack was a success.

Raids like this knocked out the three V3 launching sites that the Germans were building, so that they were never used. This saved London from terrible damage, far worse even than what it suffered.

On another occasion, "Cheese" led a raid on the E-boat moorings on the French coast. The E-boats were very fast German torpedo-boats. They had been attacking boats carrying supplies to British warships. The attack was a great success. Fourteen E-boats were destroyed, as well as nearly forty other enemy boats of various kinds.

The atomic bomb

It was the late summer of 1944. In the office of Air Vice-Marshal Cochrane sat Leonard Cheshire. Behind his desk, the older man looked at the young pilot in front of him.

"I see you've done a hundred bombing raids now."

"That's correct, sir!" replied Leonard.

"Well, that's enough. It's time you had a rest."

"A rest, sir? But I'm ..."

"It's no use arguing," the Air Vice-Marshal told him. "A hundred is a good number to stop at."

A hundred *was* a good number. The expectation of life for a bomber pilot was only twenty-five bombing raids!

Before the end of the year, Leonard had received the V.C. (Victoria Cross). This is the highest military award one can win for bravery. The award to Leonard was not for one brave action.

It was for four years of constant courage and his hundred bombing raids.

Leonard spent the next twelve months or so in a desk job. He planned bombing attacks, talked to pilots and worked for the R.A.F. in India and America, as well as in England.

He found that he now had more time to relax. He liked a drink and had two or three favourite London pubs. One day he was in one of them when he heard someone talking about God. Religion had played no part in his life up to now, yet he still felt that his view was as good as anybody else's.

"God's your conscience," he said loudly. "It tells you right from wrong, and good from bad."

"Nonsense," replied a woman. "And I'm surprised that anyone like you should say something so stupid. God's a person."

"God's one thing to some of us, another thing to others," went on Leonard, ignoring what the woman had said. "And the world would be better off without religion confusing the matter."

For quite a long time afterwards Leonard found himself wondering whether he or the woman was right. When he had nothing better to do, he thought, he would find out more about religion.

One day, a few weeks later, Leonard was asked to go and see a very important officer. He was a Field Marshal. The Field Marshal looked serious.

"I am going to tell you something that is top secret, Cheshire. In fact, this is *the* most important secret of the war."

"Yes, sir?"

"So important that I must stress the seriousness of what I'm about to tell you."

Leonard listened carefully. The Field Marshal went on to describe how an atomic bomb had been made and tested. It could blow up a whole city. The United States was going to use one against Japan. It was hoped that it would bring the war to a

An atomic bomb mushroom cloud

quick end. Two Britons were to go on the raid to see what happened. Leonard was invited to be one of the two.

The Americans were going to drop two atomic bombs on Japan. The first was to be dropped on Hiroshima. The second was to be dropped on Nagasaki. Leonard was to watch the second one.

It was 9 August 1945. In a plane, 7 or 8 miles above the Pacific Ocean, Leonard watched. He saw a flash in the sky. It was far brighter than the sun, and yet it was hundreds of miles away. A ball of fire rose from Nagasaki. Then the flame turned to a darker, cloudy colour. Where the city had been, there was just a circle of blackened earth. Everything had been destroyed.

Forty thousand people died. Some were burnt up in a second. Others died more slowly.

What was the effect on Leonard of seeing this? He felt – and he still feels – that it was right to use the bomb at that time. He believes that if the war had gone on, far more people would have been killed or injured. As it was, five days after the dropping of the atomic bombs, Japan gave in and the war was over.

However, at the same time, Leonard felt it was terrible that so many people had died. He realised that there must be better things to do in life than killing others. His bomber raids always had danger, skill and luck in them. This raid was safe and meant certain death to thousands of people.

The search for faith

Early in 1946 Leonard left the R.A.F. He tried several jobs, including running a flower shop! These jobs did not satisfy him. He wanted to do something for other people. So he wrote a series of articles for a Sunday newspaper about starting a "Colony Scheme". This was to be mainly for people who had been in the R.A.F., Army or Navy, and who had no family. The idea was for them to live together and look after each other.

Many readers sent in money to start off the Colony Scheme. Leonard was able to buy a very large house with forty-five bedrooms. It was called Gumley Hall, situated near Market Harborough, in Leicestershire. The people used their various talents to make things, grow food, cook meals and so on. They planned to share what money they earned. The trouble was that they earned very little. Some people did not work as they should have done. They lazed about. Some did not like sharing. Some got on each other's nerves. The idea had to be given up.

Gumley Hall was sold back to the person who had sold it to Leonard! However, Leonard and a few others had already set up another home. He had been able to buy this on hire purchase from an aunt.

The house was called Le Court. It was near Liss, in Hampshire. It was smaller than Gumley Hall – it had only twenty-five rooms! They tried to set up a market garden and fruit farm, but they had little success with the business. Indeed, after a year, they owed so much money that the whole idea was ended. Most of the land around the house was sold to pay off the debts.

Meanwhile, Leonard was thinking a bit more about religion. That talk in a London pub kept coming back into his mind. While at Gumley Hall he had even gone to a local church from time to time. He had also read one or two religious books.

Early in 1947 Leonard fell ill and went on a long holiday to Canada. He went to a small mountain village and stayed with an old family friend. Here the peace and quiet of the mountains and forests made him wonder if there really was a God.

When he came back, Leonard continued to live in part of Le Court. Then, one day, he heard that one of the people who had taken part in his Colony Scheme was ill in hospital.

The name of the man in hospital was Arthur Dykes. Arthur had cancer and there was nothing the doctors could do to make him better. The matron wanted Arthur to leave the hospital but could find no relative to look after him. Arthur also wanted to leave. So Leonard agreed to look around for a home for him. He did not think it would be too hard to find one somewhere. After all, the National Health Service had started and there were many charities around. However, there was no place for the dying Arthur to stay. There was only one thing he could do. He offered to take Arthur Dykes back with him to Le Court.

The doctors were surprised. After a short silence, one of them said, "He's very ill, you know. He'll need to be nursed all the time."

"I know."

"Have you had any experience of nursing people with cancer?"

"I can soon learn," answered Leonard.

So Arthur Dykes was moved to Le Court. Arthur was a Roman Catholic. His Christian faith meant much to him. It was helping him face death calmly and happily. After three months he died.

Arthur's death left many questions in Leonard's mind. How could the man be so happy when he knew he was about to die? Why had he found such peace through his prayers and the visits of his priest? Leonard picked up a book that Arthur had been reading. It was called *One Lord, One Faith*. It was about how the author had become a Roman Catholic. Leonard found that it answered many of his questions.

Reading this book, and watching the way in which Arthur had died, made Leonard very interested in religion. He talked with some priests. In the end, all this led Leonard to become a Christian. He was received into the Roman Catholic Church in December 1948.

Caring for the sick

One evening Leonard let his Bible fall open. His eye caught sight of these words: "It is better to trust in the Lord than to put confidence in man." That trust was soon to be put to the test. The telephone rang. The caller begged Leonard to take in his elderly relative who was rather frail.

Next day an ambulance arrived. Inside it was "Granny" Haynes. She was a lady of ninety-four and had to be carried out of the ambulance on a stretcher. She was fully dressed and wore her best hat! The hat had a huge feather round it. This then was Leonard's second patient.

He asked the local hospital for advice on how to nurse a bedridden, frail old woman.

"Washing's the most important thing," they told him.

"All over?" asked Leonard.

"Yes, all over," came the firm reply.

So Leonard went up to the old lady's room. She did not mind most of her clothes being taken off, or the washing. There was only one thing she did not like.

"You're not 'avin' me socks. They're not comin' off. They never 'ave."

And the "Battle of the Socks" began. Leonard won!

Leonard was sure that God wanted him to care for the sick and ill. As the news of Le Court got around the hospitals, Leonard was asked to take in many people for whom the hospitals could do no more. Some were crippled. Some were dying from an illness. Others were just old and helpless. Within a year, he was looking after between thirty and forty patients.

It was not until June 1949 that any other people worked at Le Court with Leonard Cheshire. Until then, he looked after the ill on his own. Housework was done by some of the fitter patients, and a few helped to prepare the meals. Even "Granny" Haynes peeled potatoes in bed once or twice.

Leonard did not worry too much about getting enough money to pay for looking after all these people. Some of them were able to pay for their keep and were willing to do so. Gifts of money from the public and from hospitals also helped. The flowers, holly and best vegetables from the gardens were sold. Enough money seemed to come in.

One of Leonard's first patients was an old man. He would not settle down at night without a handbell by the side of his bed. When he wanted something, he rang the bell wildly. The other patients did not like it, especially when the bell rang in the middle of the night. It woke everybody up – except Leonard!

Next door to the old man was a room full of patients suffering from T.B. (tuberculosis). Leonard decided to sleep here. Yet still he did not hear the bell. Besides, complained the patients, Leonard snored!

So, in the end, Leonard laid his bed on the floor outside the man's door. Now the old man had only to shout and Leonard would hear him. The rest of the household could sleep on in peace.

St Theresa's

Le Court was now full. The strain of caring for the ill and running the Home began to harm Leonard's health. He was often ill with flu. He was told by doctors to have a rest.

Leonard realised he needed more help. A committee was set up to look after the Home. Leonard was not sure what to do. Perhaps the Home was best left now in the care of others. Sadly, at the end of 1950, he left Le Court.

Leonard took a job with Vickers Armstrong, a large aircraft company. His job was to test a secret new aircraft, called the Swingwing. It involved flying from an old wartime airfield near Helston, in Cornwall.

A Spitfire fighter plane was fitted with the special new parts. Leonard was to test it out. He made the plane swoop high, then low, over the sea and wave-washed cliffs of Cornwall. He flew upside-down. Then he circled once or twice before coming in to land.

From one of the huts near the runway a figure in white overalls came running out.

"Everything all right, sir?"

Leonard nodded.

"Fine, thanks."

Leonard unfastened a notebook which was strapped to his knee. He had his report to make on the test flight.

Yet Leonard's mind was also on something else. He had been

asked for help by a young man called Michael. Michael had epileptic fits. No landlady would have him, and he could not go to Le Court because it was full. So Leonard invited him to stay in his own small cottage.

Not long afterwards Leonard came across Hilda. She was a woman who worked in the airfield's canteen. She was badly disabled and became very ill. Nobody seemed to care for her.

Leonard began looking for a building to start a second Home. One day, when flying above the airfield, he saw a group of old, broken-down huts on the edge of the airfield. The idea came into his mind that these huts could be turned into that Home.

He mentioned his idea to several people. They told him what they thought.

"Impossible!"
"Only fit for cows."
"No drains."
"No heating."
"You're crazy!"

With the help of local people and men from nearby Culdrose (an airfield run by the Royal Navy), Leonard's idea became a fact. He called this new Home "St Theresa's". He named it in honour of a Catholic saint by that name. He had no wish to force religion down anyone's throat. But so long as he had anything to do with it, God would be in his Homes. Soon the Home was full.

In March 1952 Leonard gave up his job with Vickers Armstrong. In the same month the Cheshire Foundation Homes for the Sick was formed as a charity. Leonard's two Homes became known as the Cheshire Homes. Although Leonard himself was a Roman Catholic, the Homes were to welcome patients of any belief.

All the extra work, however, did Leonard's health no good. One day, without warning, he collapsed. He was rushed to hospital. The doctors found that he had T.B. For over two years he was in hospital. He needed four painful operations on his lung.

Leonard Cheshire meeting one of the handicapped from overseas

On the buses

Leonard lay waiting for the first of the operations. There was a picture hanging on the wall near the foot of his bed. He found himself gazing again and again at it. It was a picture of the Holy Shroud of Turin. The Holy Shroud is said by some to be the cloth Jesus was wrapped in after He died. It has the marks of a face and body with bloodstains on it.

He looked at the face. He thought how lonely and unwanted Jesus was when He died. He thought too of all the many people who were poor or sick or sad.

"I must do more to help people," he said to himself.

For a while, Leonard considered becoming a priest or a monk. However, he felt that God wanted him to continue his work for the ill.

While recovering from T.B., Leonard had a strange idea. Before being taken ill he had hoped to go on a preaching tour, telling people of God's love. Becoming ill had stopped him. His new idea was to buy a bus and use it as a moving church – a church on wheels!

The bus was bought. It was to be seen all over England, from Yorkshire to Hampshire, from Cornwall to Kent. All round the bus were signs such as, GROUP CAPTAIN CHESHIRE'S MISSION. At the front there was a large photograph of Leonard in his R.A.F. uniform. Inside there was a crib or some other model about a Bible story. A tape-recording of Leonard talking about God could be heard. There were some chairs so that people could sit and listen to the recording or read the free religious leaflets. Booklets about the Christian faith were also sold.

Although the idea only lasted a year or two, the bus was a new way of bringing the Christian faith to ordinary people. Many who would never have bothered to listen to a sermon were willing to listen to the famous bomber pilot.

While recovering from his lung operations, Leonard also

arranged air trips for people who were ill, to a place in France called Lourdes. Some believe that miracles happen at Lourdes, through a healing spring of water. Sometimes the sick suddenly become better. Leonard himself went to Lourdes but there was no sudden cure for him. However, he came back refreshed, and sure that miracles really do happen even today.

Sue Ryder

The year 1955 was an important one for Leonard. In that year he started the first Cheshire Home overseas. It was in India. By the end of 1959 there were fifteen Cheshire Homes in Britain, six in India, one in Malaya and one in Nigeria. As well as Homes for those with incurable illnesses, there were Homes for the mentally ill, for leprosy patients, and for crippled children.

It was in 1955, too, that Leonard met Sue Ryder. In 1959 they were married. Sue has also given her life to helping those in need. She has helped thousands of people who had to leave their own countries because of war. These people are called refugees, and they sometimes have to live in refugee camps.

In 1958 Leonard and Sue set up the Ryder-Cheshire Foundation. Now it is known as "The Mission for the Relief of Suffering". The aim of this foundation is to work together on new ideas to help the suffering. For example, a group of Homes was set up in Dehra Dun in northern India. Each Home meets a particular need. There is one for the disabled, one for the mentally backward, one for orphans and one for those suffering from leprosy or TB. About 300 needy people live in this special village. A similar group of Homes has just been started in Nepal.

Some people see all the trouble and suffering in the world. Then they ask, "What is the use? What can I do? What can just one person do to help all those who suffer?"

Leonard Cheshire has given them the answer. He has found something to do, and has gone out and done it. Now there are

Part of the special village at Dehra Dun

hundreds and hundreds of people, who were once helpless and hopeless, living happy lives in his Homes.

Margaret has polio. She is very pretty, with bright eyes and dark hair. She will spend the rest of her life flat on her back in a special breathing machine.

Barbara suffers from a disease which has a long name and is difficult to say. She can only move about in a wheelchair.

David was a soldier until he was badly injured. Now he is terribly disabled.

These are just three of the hundreds of people who live in Cheshire Homes today.

The Homes are still growing in number. By 1979 there were 164. There continues to be a great need, and a lot has yet to be done. Leonard admits that the Cheshire Homes still have much to learn:

"Providing a home is simple. What is harder is to give the disabled the kind of life they should have. They should have more time on their own and be more involved in the running of the Home. Aids and gadgets help them, but we need a change of heart also. Many people still tend to look on the disabled as if they were 'simple'."

A workshop inside one of the Homes

Each of the Homes is managed by a group of local people. The day-to-day running of each Home is in the hands of a matron with three or four helpers.

One thing that stands out about Leonard Cheshire is how unselfish he is. He has now few possessions and little money compared with what he has given away. Almost all he receives is given in the service of others.

One August day in 1948, just before he died, Arthur Dykes was speaking to Leonard. Leonard was pouring disinfectant into a bowl in a corner of the sick man's room.

"Len, you'll make something good come out of this, won't you?"

Leonard smiled.

"I'll do my best, Arthur. Nothing we go through in life is lost, is it?"

The dying man in the bed sighed with pain. His long, thin fingers grasped the edge of the white sheets before he answered.

"Len, you're a saint."

BIOGRAPHICAL NOTES

Leonard Cheshire was born on 7 September 1917, at Chester. Educated at the Dragon School in Oxford, he obtained a scholarship to Stowe School in 1932. In 1936 he went to Merton College, Oxford, where he studied law.

When the Second World War began, Cheshire was posted as an R.A.F. pilot officer first to 102 Squadron and then in 1941 to 35 Squadron. He was made Wing Commander and transferred to 76 Squadron in 1942. In the following year he was promoted to Group Captain and then became a Wing Commander of 617 Squadron (the Dam Busters). He was awarded three D.S.O.s, a D.F.C. and the Victoria Cross.

In August 1945, he was an official British observer of the atomic bomb attack on Nagasaki.

In 1946 he began his V.I.P. Colony Scheme. The Cheshire Foundation Homes for the Sick was formed as a charity in March 1952.

In 1941 Cheshire married Constance Binney, an American actress who was a divorcee. The marriage was dissolved ten years later. In 1959 he married Sue Ryder, by whom he has two children – Jeremy and Elizabeth. His wife was given a life peerage in the 1978 Queen's Birthday Honours List.

THINGS TO DO

A Test yourself
Here are some short questions. See if you can remember the answers from what you have read. Then write them down in a few words.
1. Where did Leonard first have a chance to fly?
2. What did Leonard do to earn his first medal – the D.S.O.?
3. Why did Leonard prefer low-level bombing?
4. How many bombing raids did Leonard make?
5. Which country dropped two atomic bombs on Japan?
6. How did the Christian faith help Arthur Dykes?
7. How many people did Leonard care for at Le Court?
8. What is the Holy Shroud?
9. Which people in need does Sue Ryder help?
10. Who manages and runs each Cheshire Home?

B Think through
These questions need longer answers. Think about them, and then try to write two or three sentences in answer to each one. You may look up the story again to help you.
1. What were the difficulties in attacking the V3 launching sites, and how were they overcome?
2. What did Leonard feel about using the atomic bombs on Japan?
3. Why did the Colony Scheme at Gumley Hall fail?
4. What caused Leonard to become a Christian?
5. Why did Leonard buy the three buses?
6. How did Leonard find enough money to look after the patients at Le Court?

C Talk about
Here are some questions for you to talk about with each other. Try to give reasons for what you say or think. Try to find out all the different opinions which people have about each question.
1. Why do wars happen? Are they always wrong? Can any good things come out of them?
2. Leonard prayed for war to come. Was he right to do so? What things is it right to pray for? (Look up Matthew, chapter 7, verses 7–11)

3 Was it right to drop two atomic bombs on Japan without warning? Do you think that Great Britain should keep nuclear weapons or not?
4 "The world would be better off without religion." Do you agree? Why? Has religion ever done anything good for anyone?
5 Why do you think Leonard wanted to help people who were dying or disabled? Do you think his becoming a Christian had anything to do with it?

D Find out

Choose one or two or the subjects below and find out all you can about them. You will find books such as an encyclopaedia and history books useful. Your school or public library will have books on some of the subjects.

1 *The Second World War*
 (a) Which countries took part in the war? How did it start?
 (b) Find out how the Nazis came to power in Germany. What did they believe in? What did they do to the Jews, and to people who disagreed with them? (Another book in this series will help you: *The Nun in the Concentration Camp*, by G. W. Target, R.E.P.)

2 *The Royal Air Force*
 (a) Look up the history of the R.A.F.
 (b) Find out about other famous pilots such as Douglas Bader and Guy Gibson, and also about the Battle of Britain and the "Dam Busters".
 (c) Draw the different kinds of aircraft used during the Second World War.
 (d) Find out about the R.A.F. Museum at Hendon, and visit it if you can.

3 *Tuberculosis*
 (a) How do people catch this disease? How can people be protected against it?
 (b) In which countries is it still a serious problem? Why? How can it be treated?

4 *The Shroud of Turin*
 (a) When was the Turin Shroud discovered? What strange facts about it have come to light?
 (b) How far do the marks on it agree with what the Bible tells us about the suffering and death of Jesus? (Read John, chapter 19, verses 1–5, 17–40, and chapter 20, verses 4–7)

5 *Refugees*
   (a) Find out about refugees in different parts of the world. Look in newspapers and watch the news on television. Why have they had to leave their homes? Who looks after them?
   (b) Write to the address given on the next page to learn about the Sue Ryder Foundation, and what it does for refugees.
6 *Care for the dying*
   (a) What are geriatric wards in hospitals? What are hospices?
   (b) Discover all you can about Mother Teresa of Calcutta. (Another book in this series will help you: *In the Streets of Calcutta*, by Audrey Constant, R.E.P.)

USEFUL INFORMATION

Addresses
Magazines giving up-to-date information about the work of Leonard Cheshire and Sue Ryder can be obtained from:

The Leonard Cheshire Foundation
7 Market Mews
London W1Y 8HP.

The Mission for the Relief of Suffering
7 Market Mews
London W1Y 8HP.

Royal Air Force Museum
Hendon Aerodrome
London NW9 5LL.

Sue Ryder Foundation
Sue Ryder Home
Cavendish
Suffolk CO10 8AY.

For information about Mother Teresa:

Missionaries of Charity
Fernhurst
East Road
St George's Hill
Weybridge
Surrey KT13 0LG.

N.B. It is best if only one person in each class writes off for information. Remember to enclose a stamped, addressed envelope for the reply. A postal order for 50p would also be helpful, if you want plenty of material.

More books to read
How the Cheshire Homes Started, by Frank Spath (Leonard Cheshire Foundation) (P).
The Pilot Who Changed Course, by Carolyn Scott (Lutterworth) (now out of print, but available in libraries) (P).
The Turin Shroud, by Ian Wilson (Gollancz, Penguin) (T).

(T) = suitable for teachers and older pupils
(P) = suitable for younger pupils

Films
Come to Our Home (11 min), colour. Leonard Cheshire explains the work of the Homes and how children can help.
What Is a Home? (22 min), colour. An account of the daily routine in the Homes. Both films available from CTVC Film Library, Foundation House, Walton Road, Bushey, Watford WD2 2JS.

Videotapes

Challenge to Care (21 min) An account of Leonard Cheshire's war exploits and his work for the disabled.

Come to Our Home (11 min)

A Hidden World (21 min) Describes the problems of disablement and shows how many conquer their handicaps.

The Silent Witness (22 min) The story of the Holy Shroud of Turin.

All these videotapes are available for hire from the Leonard Cheshire Foundation, on either Sony or Philips cassettes, *or* from Concord Films Council, 201 Felixstowe Road, Ipswich, Suffolk IP3 9BJ, on Philips cassettes.